I Am Older Than Most of You!

Delights and Doubts of A Nonagenarian

by Ruth P. Arent

Sketches by Sally Arent McCain

Poems are a treat for all ages. Let my poetry offer you a pathway between the part of you which chatters and that which is listening, gifting you with a connection to yourself and to others.

http://www.rutharent.com

Illustrations: Sally Arent McCain

Editing and compilation by Dianne Roth
"Hog Island Pine" sketch: DianneDesigns
dianneroth.com/diannedesigns.html

Arent, Ruth P.
 I am older than most of you! :
 Delights and Doubts of a Nonagenarian / Ruth P. Arent

ISBN: 978-0-692-21282-0

Published: 2014, Corvallis, Oregon
All rights reserved.

Table of Contents

Greetings	1
Bugs... Bugs... Bugs	3
Welcome Each Day	4
My New Best Friend..My iPad	5
Apologies - Directive for my generation	6
Life's Imperfections	7
Two Umbrellas	8
Slippage	9
Lessons From Leaves	10
Gee Whiz! A Quiz!	11
Consternation	12
Thank you.. Where have you Gone?	13
Repositioning... From the Cutting Edge To Observer... Child Therapy, My World	14
My Home in Maine... Hog Island	15
My Digestive Serenade	16
Lucky Me	17
Civil Rights... Where Have They Gone?	18
Imaginary Playmates	19
Good Morning, Memory	20
We All Do It!	21
My Private Mission	22
The Old Boat	23
Birthday Party Greeting, 2012	24
Escalator Woes	26
A Favorite Poem	27

Bugs...Bugs...Bugs

My parents were proud of their buggies.
They spoke of their horses and such.
I have a collection of bugs
That I do not admire or clutch.

   It bugs me when my words get befuddled.
   It bugs me when memory stalls.
   It bugs me when "Should haves" take over.
   It bugs me when energy falls.

     My days are supposed to go smoothly
     And sleep be a wonderful treat.
     So, it bugs me when I've been unproductive
     Or I feel some task's incomplete.

       It bugs me that I feel ineffective
       In this turbulent world of today.
       It bugs me when folks use denial
       Of facts to threaten, persuade or betray.

          It bugs me that anything bugs me at all.
          Why can't I be all time accepting
          Of those who surround me
              ... human nature at large...
          And stop wishing, hoping, expecting?

          I promise myself to keep trying
          My bugs to exterminate.
          To become the person I want to be.
          Better hurry before it's too late!

Welcome Each Day

Each day holds delight
And supports my intention
To search for the light
That comes from attentions
And comes from dear smiles,
And ignore the unpleasant,
The worries and trials,
And stay in the present.

    Each day I welcome
    The tasks to be done.
    Some will be hard work
    And some will be fun.
    Relax. Not a single test to take
    And little need to stress.
    Whenever I want, I can take a break.
    I can be tidy or just leave a mess.

Perhaps it takes longer to finish my work.
But, how truly grateful I am
That I don't go berserk!
And each day is an offering
Of choices to make -
My chance to be upbeat
For everyone's sake!

My New Best Friend...

We spend hours together each day.
    I marvel at every display.
        It answers my questions and doubts,
        Points out places of interest and routes.

        DNA is not a new auto,
        RNA not an airline or med.
        Is nano the new word for Nanny,
        Or factual science instead?

    The games that we play are addictive,
    The puzzles we solve friendly too.
    And the pictures of family and places
    Need daily inspection. That's true.

The breadth and excitement of YouTube
    Is ready whenever I choose.
    And music is in every genre,
    Or perhaps it is time for the news.

So here's to my steady companion,
    Loyal guardian of my aging brain.
    Correcting mistakes that I make,
    You teach, create, entertain.
You're the newest best friend that I ever had,
    Thank you, thank you, my iPad.

Apologies --
A Directive For My Generation

Consider the sharing of musings
About noteworthy trends today.
I feel we should say we are sorry,
We're shifting huge problems their way.

Sit back and study what we bequeath
To young persons, the leaders some day.
Look hard at the surface and what lies beneath
And ponder how things went astray.

Details of inventions, yes enrichments galore,
Computers, space quests, and energy schemes.
Alas, unthinkable weapons of war,
And assess what all of this means.

Applaud what is great but regard the whole scene.
I think we might well be ashamed
Of the turmoil, destruction, anguish unseen
We created, ignored or inflamed.

We've taught many, too many, to be selfish.
One mantra... so simple, so plain.
Look out for yourself, go be greedy,
No need to be coy or explain.

Consider the sharing of musings
About noteworthy trends of today.
I feel we should say we are sorry
We're shifting huge problems their way.

Life's Imperfections

Holy Moses!
A new diagnosis
To add to my current collection.

Big long name
But not the same
'Cause this is for infection.

Medical terms
Make me squirm
I puzzle with conjection.

I am befuddled
Am I in trouble?
A natural projection.

Oh, what the hell.
I will not dwell
Or try to make connections.

Addicted to hope
It helps me cope
It's not based on deception,

But a firm mental stand
Rehearsed and planned
With serious reflections,

To use wisdom and strength
And go to all lengths
When faced with life's imperfections.

Two Umbrellas

Be very careful where you stand,
Overhead two umbrellas beckon.
One casts endless warnings
Of calamities it reckons.

"You may fall and break a hip
So a walker may be needed."
"Driving is beyond absurd!"
Warnings constantly repeated.

An endless drone that drives me nuts
Like old age at its worst.
I avoid this parasol.
My patience... it may burst.

The other is SO different,
Drops of cheerfulness come thru.
Plans to make and friends to see,
Acquaintances renew.
"Keep your sense of humor."
"Nap as often as you wish."
"Dwelling on bad news and threats
Is simply not your dish."

Tis attitude, my friends,
The umbrellas set the stage.
And I'm beneath the upbeat one
It IS befitting for my age.

Slippage

Went to school in a dress with a slip underneath.
I slipped on the ice. Not hurt. A relief!
Made a Freudian slip and I even blushed,
Should have been quiet. Discretely hushed.

Even though I am naughty, when I am able
I'll slip the dog a bit from the table.
So I do not fall on the slippery floor
I slip into my slippers to be steady, for sure.

But <u>memory</u> <u>slippage</u> is not fun, ...not one bit!
Frankly, it's annoying, but I can't make it quit!

Lessons from Leaves

When a leaf falls from a tree it does not despair.
It enjoys its free-fall journey thru the air.
What a great example leaves portray for us.
To progress - to move without a fuss.

A leaf enjoys sunshine, the wind, and the rain,
Thoughts of the future, not in its domain.
Can **we** make transitions as smoothly as that?
What about problems we have to combat?

As the leaf descends, it seems at peace.
There's no struggle, ...its nature at ease.
The message it portrays, we must emulate.
Welcome changes ...there's no early, there's no late.

As the ground below welcomes the gift of each leaf,
May we try to be tranquil and display the belief
That new scenes denote progress, if you will.
So we'll share our gifts and strive to fulfill
Our lives with pleasures, midst lessons to learn,
Not let fear, greed, or anger be of major concern.

Once more, picture the leaf on its quiet descent.
It models a calmness that is meant
For us to adopt as we cope and mature,
And seek brightness and wisdom in all we endure.
This calmness translates into choices we make
In all that we shall undertake.

As one ages, one thought is clear,
Nature proffers changes, year after year.
Quietly and gently each stage arrives,
So all may bud, hatch, grow, and thrive.
Nature endows us with energy, too.
And spirit and challenges to pursue.

Gee Whiz! A Quiz!

Gee whiz! A quiz for you!
Who were two friends of Winnie the Pooh?
Did you name Piglet or Eeyore or Roo?
Now wasn't that a fun thing to do?

And seven dwarfs were with Snow White.
It was many kids' delight.
Which of the names come to light?
Sleepy, Grumpy, Doc, ...no, ...not Bright.
Did you get the seven right?

Now Santa made visits. Can you name his crew?
They flew Xmas Eve, the whole night thru.
There's Dancer, and Vixen, and Comet, a few.
The others? ...you'll have to Google that, too!

Consternation

I am angry, yes indeed.
I cannot fathom corporate greed.
To be successful, I applaud
Successful works here and abroad.
But disrespect for workers? NO!
They are not robots, ...kept in tow.
But folks with feelings, hopes and strengths
Willing to try and go great lengths
To measure up and to comply,
Trusting that soon, not by and by,
Their future will be guaranteed.
But let's get real, they can't succeed
When underpaid, or out the door,
Disrespected, and much more.

They're victimized by corporate chiefs.
Folks who hold the cold beliefs
That money rules while folks don't count.
And this infects, upsets, amounts
To the statement, "That's how it is.
Inequality.
Bottom line, reality."

I say, "NO" it's so unfair.
And I am edging towards despair,
Forecasting things are getting worse.
Better end this poignant verse.

"Thank you" Where have you gone?

Please tell me where "Thank you" is hiding?
Is it scrunched 'neath a tree or a log?
Have some folks forgotten to bring it along
When walking or out for a jog?

When someone moves over to get out of the way,
Then what's the polite thing to say?
"Thank you" of course, ...without any doubt.
This politeness is missing today.

And presents are given to please and delight
With thoughtfulness, time, and some cash.
Should one expect a "Thank you" in time,
Or is that old fashioned or brash?

A "Thank you" is welcome like a smile or a tip.
A "Thank you" acknowledges aid.
"Thank you" is proper each child is told.
It's a compliment freely conveyed.

Don't fail to explain what is proper and kind
And, for bonding with those you hold dear,
"Thank you" is basic and rudeness must go.
Take care to use words that endear.

Repositioning
...from the Cutting Edge to Observer...
Child Therapy, my World

Now I am outside looking in
Since new approaches did begin.
My thoughts quite often go adrift
As my life has had to make the shift
From being on the cutting edge,
From leading from a careful ledge
Of strategies and methods too,
For helping children, which were new,
To feeling old and left behind.
Oh time, indeed, may be unkind!

I pioneered the doll play schemes
To help learn underlying themes
That children struggled and endured
So they would feel more self assured.

I modeled openness and trust.
Revealing self ...a novel must.
Established as child's advocate
And parents were aware of that.

With finger paints and modeling clay,
Or music, books, ---most anyway
To help the children better cope
And feel empowered, welcome hope.

Tender topics handled, yes
Tho some I missed, I must confess.
But all in all a great career
Which warrants glimpses from the rear.

Today, the fine work on the brain
Contributes much to salve the pain
As therapists select both old and new
I hail them all, there are too few.

My Home in Maine... Hog Island

Have you ever read a book that inspired you to write?
Anne Morrow Lindbergh's "Gift from the Sea"
    inspired me tonight.
As she strolled on the beach, she had nothing to fear
She was pensive and quiet,
    her thoughts poignant and clear.
She was peaceful, relaxed, her ideas profound
With the waves and the shells,
    she let nature abound.

My home in Maine
    is where I retreat.
It welcomes my being,
    I feel so complete.

Rippling water,
    the trees on the path
The rain drops that happily
    give rocks a bath,
The squirrels and loons
    that make certain I know
They're sending greetings,
    as they come and go.

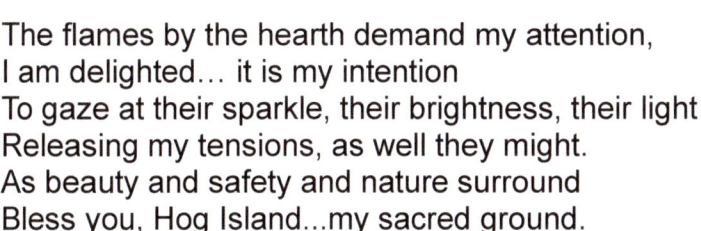

    The flames by the hearth demand my attention,
    I am delighted… it is my intention
    To gaze at their sparkle, their brightness, their light
    Releasing my tensions, as well they might.
    As beauty and safety and nature surround
    Bless you, Hog Island…my sacred ground.

A Digestive Serenade

I have a new attraction
It is called the "stomach rumble".
Untrained melody for sure.
Played by a gaseous ensemble.
I picture water bumping 'gainst rock
Then the squeak of a curious bird.
These are some of the strangest sounds
That I have ever heard.

I hope this serenade does not persist.
Tho amusing, and distracting,
It commands my attention,
The organs are contracting!
But tummy sounds are not polite
And may forewarn disaster.
They ignite my worry machine.
Meanwhile, nature is my music master .

Lucky Me

Luck is not a four leaf clover
Luck is here and there – all over
If you search you will uncover,
I share with you what I've discovered.

Professors whom I did revere
Led me to a great career
I pursued year after year
Lucky me.

One son, daughters three
Talented and caring
My special family,
Lucky me.

As a Grammie, I declare
My grandkids are beyond compare
Happily their news they share,
Lucky me.

Travels, opportunity
To visit life-long friends, you see
As well as splendid scenery,
Lucky me.

Raging Grannies, friends indeed
Wonderful activity
Singing loud where we should be,
Lucky me.

Happily I've got energy
Able to hear and smile and see
Blessed with a working memory,
Very lucky me.

Civil Rights... Where Have They Gone?
(Lyrics for a Raging Granny song to the tune:
Oh Where, Oh Where has my Little Dog Gone?)

Oh where, oh where have our civil rights gone?
Oh where oh where can they be?
With our freedoms cut short,
In and out of the court,
Oh what is our future to be?

Oh where oh where have our workers rights gone?
Some unions are under the knife.
They struggled for ages,
To bargain for wages,
And jobs for the rest of their lives.

Our protests and free speech are under attack
On Wall Street and Murdoch TV.
The folks on the street,
They were maced and were beat,
More symptoms of corporate greed.

Oh why, oh why must we Grannies sing?
Oh why, oh why must we rage?
Because there's a need,
To stop the stampede,
Let civil rights take center stage!

Imaginary Playmates

Some wee folks have imaginary playmates.
Some very old folks too!
Little ones tell of wild places they've been,
Oh, the wonders they construe.

Now the plentiful wrinkles that rest on old legs
And those that adorn every arm
Offer me endless channels and spots
For tales to amuse and alarm.

One path on my leg is clearly the street
That played host to Oliver Twist.
Another is windy where Paul Revere rode.
This is true. I insist! I insist!

The spots on the skin are the most fun of all
They are fires or ink drops or lakes.
But no one but me has a name for my spots
And I never can make a mistake!

A charming, tangled web,
'T would swell a spider's pride.
And it lives below my elbow,
Where its host can safely hide.

I watch the blood travel veins on my hand.
I push it right back just for fun.
I know that some masses of wrinkles have come
From the years I played in the sun.

So don't distress if lumpy veins
Are scribbled on your arms.
It's nature's customized design
To entertain and charm.

Good Morning, Memory

Does your memory flip flop
When you're wide awake at dawn?
Are you perky, set to start the day?
Or, does coffee launch your morn?

Whatever your pattern,
Whatever your style,
Does your memory flip flop,
Spin around for a while?

This very morning
While still in my bed,
Four batches of memories
Switched about in my head.

The first had to do with some treasures I'd loved.
Two Teddy bears made by Steiff
Sat on my bed for many a year,
Security blanket, dear parts of my life.

Then an autograph book with a zipper,
Each camp friend had scribbled a thought.
Some ribbons I'd won in some swim meets,
A sweater, handmade and not bought.

The third memory partition
Abounds in dids and did nots.
Some were delightful and some I regret,
Some straightened, some tied in knots.

Then Brain flops over to nature,
Such contrast to people and things.
Welcome the smells, scenes, and beauty,
And wonders that non-humans bring.

This memory bombardment confuses
When the issues of today, thin or deep,
Are abruptly brought to attention...
Too much! ...better go back to sleep!

We All Do It!

Billy Crystal said it first
I think it's worth repeat.
He told his folks
"This meal's on me,"
When they went out to eat.

And so it was he spilled and spilled,
On trousers and on shirt.
His drink and food, from soup to nuts,
Including the dessert.

So when your food slips off your fork
Or ice cream spots your chin,
Enjoy your meal, the company,
And let the mess begin.

My Private Mission

I have a private mission in tow –
Supporting soul wherever I go.
What does this mean? I'm not being coy.
It means I'm determined to bring about joy
To others – no matter the time or the scene.
Help overcome fear or some sadness unseen.

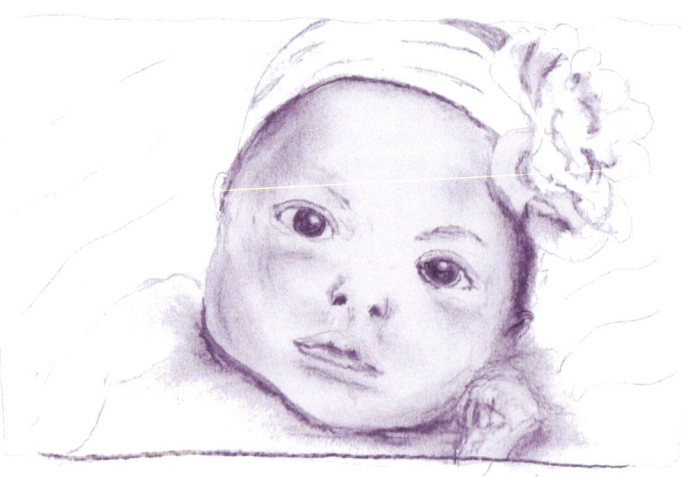

It is my understanding, all babies at birth
Are blessed with a soul – the root of self-worth,
Which provides a lifelong reserve of good will.
I'll tap **my** reserve to help others fulfill
Their needs or their wants – tho reluctant to ask.
I'll share my joy and lightness -
My mission, my task.

The Old Boat

What a wondrous collection of treasures and stuff
To amaze my inquisitive mind.
Old oil cans and varnish and
Rusty machines
That no longer grind.

    Speak up, ancient friend and tell me the tales
    Of what occurred when you were afloat.
    Did lovers make out or fishermen swear?
    Did you take explorers to coves quite remote
    So they could be pirates or villains so bad?
    What other adventures have you ever had?

Your belly is scratched, your paint a bit dull
Your essence of "come aboard" is feeble, but well.
You hunger for action, I can tell by your perch,
You yearn for the water in order to search
For new docks and landings that appear on the shore.
And I hear your plea, "I am old, but want more!"

    I'm sorry my friend ...too hard to repair.
    But you must rejoice... I still really care.
    I'll come and touch you, once in a while,
        And reflect for a minute and quietly smile.

Birthday Party Greetings
My greetings to friends and family
at my 90th birthday party,
March, 2012

I will tell you something seriously
How I got to ninety is a mystery.
I remember as a kid sledding on the hill
My brothers had to rescue me after every spill.
Learning to write and read, I still picture,
But even today my poor math is a mixture
Of numbers and lines and concepts befuddling.
So I just pretend that I get it and stop struggling.

Now, school days were happy while I was at school
Or when working out in a welcoming pool.
I had a collection of jobs that were fun
Those adorable toddlers. I loved every one!

College was ok, but I have to admit,
At Skidmore it was cliquey and I didn't fit.
But graduate schools were the right spots for me
So much to learn, ...about life, ...about me.

'Twas during the war, and important reflections
About all values and all my connections.
It was not hard to sense how everyone felt,
And decisions, ...I voted for Roosevelt...
Were upheld by commitments sincere
Which I reaffirmed, year after year.

Life was full – tasks aplenty,
But things blossomed for me in my twenties.
Studies, and research, and marriage to Jack.
Such happy memories ...smiles to look back.
Then special bundles ...four kids on the scene,
Great times ...sad times ... and times in between.

MY life, ... scrambled eggs on a plate
Each ingredient added flavor, no matter the date
Of adventure, experience, jobs done or not,
Of people and places which just hit the spot.

As a therapist and a speaker
My work was a wondrous affair.
My friendships I have cherished
And handled with care.

Now I'll wax sentimental a moment or three
And offer some thoughts that are fervent to me.
Some new ones, some old ones, some preachy, perhaps,
Bearing in mind, ...big pieces or scraps.

If you were to read the books on my shelf,
Many declare, "Be good to yourself."
This is a message of major concern,
One that takes year after year to learn.

You are unique, your talents to show.
So just be yourself wherever you go.
Take notice of people whose traits you admire,
Then create your persona, ...no lessons required.

Escalator Woes

I jumped back. I couldn't take the step.

The moving stairs, ...they went so fast

I took a breath, ...then grasped the rail

Like a toddler, ...scared and frail.

My brain scolded, "You sissy! You!"

The lady behind me sighed.

But I thought I would stumble,

Too ashamed to mumble.

I stared at the moving stairs once more,

Befriended the yellow stripes.

They beckoned me to come aboard.

I tried!!! And up those stairs I soared!

In Some Way, However Small and Secret
By Leo Rosten

In some way, however small and secret,
each of us is a little mad.
Everyone is lonely at bottom and cries to be understood.
But we can never entirely understand someone else, and
Each of us remains part stranger, even to those who love us.
It is the weak who are cruel.
Gentleness can only be expected from the strong.
Those who do not know fear are not really brave,
For courage is the capacity to confront what can be imagined.
And you can understand people better if you look at them,
No matter how old or impressive they are,
As if they are children.
For most of us never really mature, we simply grow taller.
And happiness comes only when we push our hearts
And brains to the farthest reaches of which we are capable.
But the purpose of life is to matter, to count,
To stand for something,
    To have it make some difference that we lived at all.

                    ~~ My favorite poem,
                        I hope you enjoy it.
                            ~~ Ruth

www.ingramcontent.com/pod-product-compliance
Lightning Source LLC
Chambersburg PA
CBHW041746040426
42444CB00004B/187